D1128155

THE RADIO CITY
ROCKETTES
A DANCE THROUGH TIME

PHOTOGRAPHS BY

MSG
ENTERTAINMENT

JAMES PORTO

The Radio City Rockettes: A Dance through Time.
© 2006 MSG Entertainment, a division of Madison Square Garden, L.P.
"Rockettes," "Radio City Rockettes," "Radio City," "Radio City Music Hall,"
"Radio City Christmas Spectacular," and "Christmas Spectacular" are registered
trademarks of Radio City Trademarks LLC. All rights reserved. Printed in the
United States of America. No part of this book may be used or reproduced
in any manner whatsoever without written permission except in the case of
brief quotations embodied in critical articles and reviews. For information,
address HarperCollins Publishers, 10 East 53rd Street, New York, NY 10022.
James Porto Photographs: © 2006 James Porto Photography, Inc. and MSG
Entertainment, a division of Madison Square Garden, L.P. All rights reserved.

HarperCollins books may be purchased for educational, business,
or sales promotional use. For information, please write:
Special Markets Department, HarperCollins Publishers,
10 East 53rd Street, New York, NY 10022.

First edition

Interior design by Kathleen Burchell
Photographs supplied by James Porto, MSG Entertainment, and
George Kalinsky for Madison Square Garden

Printed on acid-free paper

Library of Congress Cataloging-in-Publication Data is available upon request.

ISBN 10: 0-06-134114-2

06 07 08 09 10 /UNG 10 9 8 7 6 5 4 3 2 1

CONTENTS

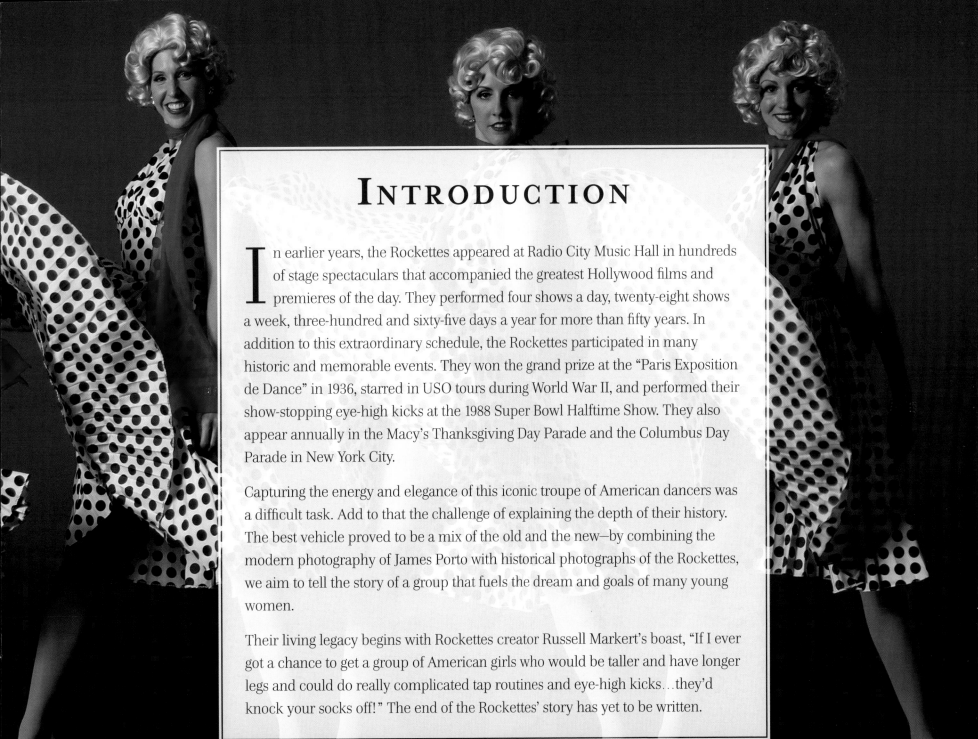

INTRODUCTION

In earlier years, the Rockettes appeared at Radio City Music Hall in hundreds of stage spectaculars that accompanied the greatest Hollywood films and premieres of the day. They performed four shows a day, twenty-eight shows a week, three-hundred and sixty-five days a year for more than fifty years. In addition to this extraordinary schedule, the Rockettes participated in many historic and memorable events. They won the grand prize at the "Paris Exposition de Dance" in 1936, starred in USO tours during World War II, and performed their show-stopping eye-high kicks at the 1988 Super Bowl Halftime Show. They also appear annually in the Macy's Thanksgiving Day Parade and the Columbus Day Parade in New York City.

Capturing the energy and elegance of this iconic troupe of American dancers was a difficult task. Add to that the challenge of explaining the depth of their history. The best vehicle proved to be a mix of the old and the new—by combining the modern photography of James Porto with historical photographs of the Rockettes, we aim to tell the story of a group that fuels the dream and goals of many young women.

Their living legacy begins with Rockettes creator Russell Markert's boast, "If I ever got a chance to get a group of American girls who would be taller and have longer legs and could do really complicated tap routines and eye-high kicks…they'd knock your socks off!" The end of the Rockettes' story has yet to be written.

THE ROCKETTES TODAY

The modern-day Rockettes play an integral role in many MSG Entertainment productions and special events. They've tapped their way through the dreams of thousands of young girls, many of whom hope to one day add their legs to that world–famous kick line.

So you want to be a Rockette? Open auditions are held annually and hundreds of women answer the call. Rockettes must be between 5'6" and 5'10½" and must demonstrate proficiency in tap, jazz, ballet, and modern dance. They need to display a radiant energy that will shine across the footlights to their audience. Rockettes must also be able to sing and, of course, perform those eye-high kicks.

"A Rockette performance may look simple to the audience, but it's really very intricate. A lot of it is counting in your head," says Rockette legend Muriel "Duffey" Kilduff Hake.

The lounges of Radio City Music Hall are plush, elegant, and serve as mini-galleries that house some very significant works of art.

The walls of the Grand Lounge (right) feature the works of Louis Bouche, titled *The Phantasmagoria of the Theatre*, depicting the past and present of the stage in five vignettes.

The Grand Foyer was designed by Donald Deskey.
The bronze plaques, designed by Rene Chambellan, that decorate these stainless-steel doors represent different eras of theatre found in the history of various nations.

MEET THE ROCKETTES

The Rockettes have been described as a team of dancers moving as one. Their costumes are always the same. The dance line is carefully planned so that the women appear to be the same height. It's easy to forget, that behind these seamless precision moves, are individuals.

Hailing from all over the country, these skilled athletes and dancers are the living legacy of Rockettes founder Russell Markert's original glamorous gals. Photographer James Porto captures their unique beauty as they model costumes from the Radio City Music Hall archives.

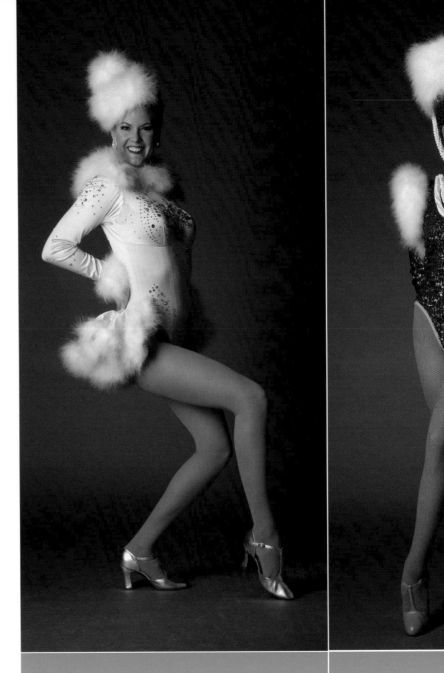

NAME: CHERYL CUTLIP

BORN: HIGH POINT, NC

COSTUME: SNOWFLAKE 1989
PETE MENEFEE

NAME: AMY KARLEIN

BORN: ERIE, PA

COSTUME: SEQUINS AND FUR (RED) 198
PETE MENEFEE

NAME: MORNING-STAR MOSLEY

BORN: LONG BEACH, CA

COSTUME: SINGING IN THE RAIN 1996
FRANK KRENZ

NAME: AMY LOVE OSGOOD

BORN: CORDOVA, AK

COSTUME: CANDY CANE BIZZAZZ 1999
PETE MENEFEE

NAME: HANNAH ELLINGTON SIDES

BORN: WESTMINISTER, MA

COSTUME: SNOWFLAKE 1989
PETE MENEFEE

NAME: CHRISTINA HEDRICK

BORN: RICHMOND, VA

COSTUME: GOLD & RHINESTONES 1977
FRANK SPENCER

NAME: CALLIE CARTER

BORN: LOMBARD, IL

COSTUME: TAPPING SAILORS 1983
LINDSAY DAVIS

NAME: LINDSAY BISCHOFF

BORN: DAYTON, OH

COSTUME: ROCKETTE RED SANTA 1982
PETE MENEFEE

NAME: CYNTHIA-MARGEAUX MULLER

BORN: LONG ISLAND, NY

COSTUME: HUNNY BUNNY 1996
GREGG BARNES

NAME: SAMANTHA BERGER

BORN: YORKTOWN, VA

COSTUME: CITY RHYTHM 1999
DEBORAH NEWHALL

NAME: KARA MARIE SANDBERG

BORN: RANCHO PALOS VERDES, CA

COSTUME: VELVET MARCH 1999
DEBORAH NEWHALL

THE 1920s

Under the supervision of their founder, Russell Markert, the Radio City Rockettes began kicking up their heels in 1925, dazzling audiences with their exactness, precision, and uniformity. They were first known as the "Missouri Rockets" and made their show debut in St. Louis. The same year, the troupe traveled to New York City to perform in the Broadway show *Rain or Shine*. S. L. "Roxy" Rothafel hired the troupe to perform at the Roxy Theatre and renamed them the Roxyettes. The women then moved off the stage and into the movies, appearing in *Animal Crackers* and *The King of Jazz*.

Starting with just sixteeen women, over the years the troupe grew to a line of thirty-six dancers.

Russell Markert

Russell Markert created the exemplary American chorus line—an exciting precision dance company with great style, flair, and glamour. His inspiration was the John Tiller girls of the 1922 Ziegfeld Follies.

Markert's stringent requirements never varied, and he continued to stage and choreograph productions at the Music Hall until his retirement in 1971.

His concept of the dance line was to achieve absolute precision and ultimate uniformity in the movements of the dancers. The audience saw thirty-six Rockettes perform intricate routines, but always moving as "one dancer." Everything—from the costumes to the specific steps—was kept completely identical. The illusion of uniform height has always been maintained by having the tallest dancers in the center of the line and placing dancers of gradually decreasing height on either side, with the shortest women at both ends of the line.

S. L. "Roxy" Rothafel

The Missouri Rockets were in New York City rehearsing to perform in the Broadway show *Rain or Shine* when they were discovered by consummate showman S. L. "Roxy" Rothafel. Their New York debut was in the Roxy Theatre on 50th Street and Seventh Avenue. "The Rockets" were so much of an instant hit that Rothafel was loathe to let them leave. He pleaded with Russell Markert to form another line to replace the departing Rockets.[1] There were actually three separate Rocket dance troupes performing in New York at the time.

Rothafel moved two of the troupes to Radio City Music Hall for opening night in 1932. He first dubbed them the "Roxyettes." In 1934, the Roxyettes officially become the Radio City Music Hall Rockettes.

NAME: AMY LING

BORN: ROCHESTER, NY

COSTUME: CITY RHYTHM 1999
DEBORAH NEWHALL

NAME: SIOBHAN SANATPAOLA

BORN: GLEN COVE, NY

COSTUME: CHRISTMAS STAR 2005
GREGG BARNES

NAME: LINDSAY HOWE

BORN: SACRAMENTO, CA

COSTUME: GERSHWIN DIAMOND 1990
ERTÉ

NAME: KELLY KING

BORN: GOSHEN, NY

COSTUME: MIRROR 2003
GREGG BARNES

NAME: NICOLE BATALIAS

BORN: WOOD RIDGE, NJ

COSTUME: REINDEER 1999
GREGG BARNES

NAME: CHRISTINE SIENICKI

BORN: PASSAIC, NJ

COSTUME: HOT PINK TUXEDO 1978
FRANK SPENCER

NAME: HALEY BENIK MORGAN

BORN: MYRTLE BEACH, SC

COSTUME: HOT PINK TUXEDO 1978
FRANK SPENCER

NAME: MELINDA FARRELL

BORN: WASHINGTON, DC

COSTUME: CHRISTMAS CAROUSEL 1989
LEEANNE MITCHELL

NAME: JEN WERNER

BORN: ROCK HILL, SC

COSTUME: VELVET MARCH 1999
DEBORAH NEWHALL

NAME: NIKKI LONG

BORN: POMONA, CA

COSTUME: TAPPING SAILORS 1983
LINDSAY DAVIS

NAME: KAT STEERS

BORN: MONTCLAIR, NJ

COSTUME: GOLD SWIRL 2001
GREGG BARNES

NAME: DANIELLE MATHEWS

BORN: HACKENSACK, NJ

COSTUME: RED, WHITE, & BLUE POOF 1981
FRANK SPENCER

Y
MUSIC
HALL
CADILLAC CONCERT SERIES
MARK KNOPFLER
JUNE 29
Music Hall
RADIO CITY
NE 29 AT 8PM
BACKSTREET BOYS JULY 27 ON SALE NOW
Subway

RADIO CITY MUSIC HALL

When the stock market crashed in 1920, most people tried to hold on to whatever money that they had left. Contrary to public sentiment, John D. Rockefeller made the bold decision to build an entire complex of buildings.

Rockefeller's financial power and Radio Corporation of America's media might were joined by the impresario S. L. "Roxy" Rothafel. Roxy had earned a reputation as a theatrical genius by employing an innovative combination of vaudeville, movies, and razzle-dazzle décor to revive struggling theatres across America. Together they realized a fantastic dream—a theatre unlike any in the world. It was a palace for the people, a place of beauty offering high-quality entertainment at prices ordinary people could afford. It was intended to entertain and amuse, but also to elevate and inspire. It was Radio City Music Hall.

A contest was held to select the designer for the Music Hall's interior. Donald Deskey wasn't the most celebrated designer in the competition; in fact, he was relatively unknown. Deskey's designs chose elegance over excess, grandeur above glitz. He designed more than thirty separate spaces, including eight lounges and smoking rooms, each with its own motif. Art was an integral part of the design. Fine artists created murals, wall coverings, and sculptures; textile designers developed draperies and carpets; craftsmen made ceramics, wood panels, and chandeliers. Everything about it was larger than life. Although it was built in 1932, the Art Deco style of the Music Hall is still fresh today.

Radio City Music Hall's marquee is a full city-block long.

It is the largest indoor theatre in the world, with an auditorium that is 160 feet from back to stage and a ceiling that reachs a height of 84 feet. The walls and ceilings are formed by a series of sweeping arches that define a splendid and immense curving space.

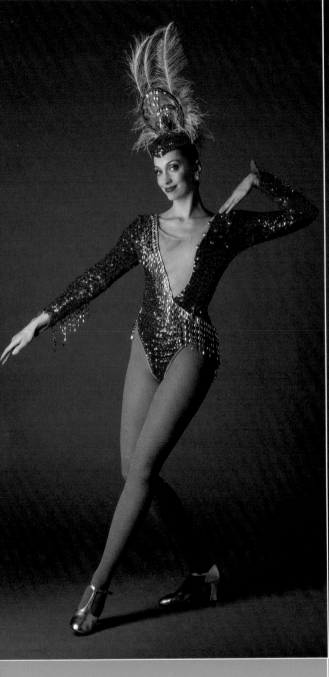

NAME: KRISTIN MARIE JOHNSON

BORN: FORT LAUDERDALE, FL

COSTUME: RED SEQUIN WITH FRINGE 1977
FRANK SPENCER

NAME: MICHELE IMOR-DRAXLER

BORN: CLIFTON, NJ

COSTUME: SILVER FEATHER FINALE 1990
ERTÉ

NAME: BETH DUKLETH

BORN: HOUSTON, TX

COSTUME: PURPLE USHERETTE 2001
JACK MCGRODER

NAME: Karida Griffith

BORN: Portland, OR

COSTUME: Hot Pink Tuxedo 1978
Frank Spencer

NAME: Krista Saab

BORN: Toronto, Canada

COSTUME: Singing in the Rain 1996
Frank Krenz

NAME: Kandice Pelletier

BORN: Lubbock, TX

COSTUME: Silver Feather Finale 1990
Erté

NAME: MELISSA HILLMER

BORN: LANCASTER, WI.

COSTUME: VELVET MARCH 1999

DEBORAH NEWHALL

NAME: EMILY STACKS

BORN: CENTREVILLE, VA

COSTUME: SAILOR 1984

MICHAEL CASEY

NAME: ALISON LEVENBERG

BORN: NORWICH, ENGLAND

COSTUME: HOT PINK TUXEDO 1978

FRANK SPENCER

NAME: SHERI GRIFFITH-DAGUE

BORN: PITTSBURGH, PA

COSTUME: ORANGE MIRROR 1977
FRANK SPENCER

NAME: CAITIE MCCARTHY

BORN: POUGHKEEPSIE, NY

COSTUME: SNOWFLAKE 1989
PETE MENEFEE

NAME: KRISTEN FOOTE

BORN: TORONTO, CANADA

COSTUME: SINGING IN THE RAIN 1996
FRANK KRENZ

NAME: KIM CALORE-SEDLAK

BORN: WARWICK, RI

COSTUME: CHRISTMAS STAR 2005
GREGG BARNES

NAME: MELISSA FAGAN

BORN: ST. LOUIS, MO

COSTUME: GOLD & RHINESTONES 1977
FRANK SPENCER

NAME: ALANA NIEHOFF

BORN: AURORA, CO

COSTUME: RED FIREWORKS 1981
FRANK SPENCER

NAME: Jaime Lyn Windrow

BORN: Coventry, RI

COSTUME: Gershwin Diamond 1990
Erté

NAME: Rhonda Kaufman Malkin

BORN: Phoenix, AZ

COSTUME: Bells 1987
Pete Menefee

NAME: Amanda Suchy

BORN: Lexington, KY

COSTUME NAME: Purple Usherette 2001
Jack McGroder

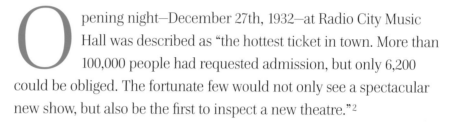

THE 1930s

Opening night—December 27th, 1932—at Radio City Music Hall was described as "the hottest ticket in town. More than 100,000 people had requested admission, but only 6,200 could be obliged. The fortunate few would not only see a spectacular new show, but also be the first to inspect a new theatre."[2]

The show was scheduled to start at 9 P.M. "The opening night program documents the size of what must have been the biggest variety or vaudeville show in history. Nineteen separate acts were scheduled. Nobody involved remembers the precise running time, but all agree that it was painfully long."[3]

The Roxyettes shared the stage with other acts including the Flying Wallendas, Ray Bolger (who would become famous in the role of the Scarecrow in *The Wizard of Oz),* and choreographer Martha Graham.

The Roxyettes' dance number was to the song "With a Feather in Your Cap." Their perfect precision won over the opening night crowd.

In 1939, the Rockettes perform at the New York World's Fair (right).

Just two weeks after its gala opening, Radio City Music Hall premiered its first film, *The Bitter Tea of General Yen*. Radio City quickly became the favorite first-run theatre for moviemakers and moviegoers alike. Before long, a first showing at the Music Hall virtually guaranteed a successful run in theatres around the country.

Since 1933 more than seven hundred movies have opened at the Music Hall. They include the original *King Kong, National Velvet, White Christmas, Mame, Breakfast at Tiffany's, To Kill a Mockingbird, Mary Poppins, 101 Dalmatians,* and *The Lion King*. Radio City Music Hall featured a new movie every week accompanied by a lavish and unique stage production starring the Rockettes.

NAME: TEMPLE KANE

BORN: HANOVER, PA

COSTUME: GERSHWIN BOA 1990
ERTÉ

NAME: PURDIE BAUMANN

BORN: MAYWOOD, IL

COSTUME: DANCING IN DIAMONDS 1982
BOB MACKIE

NAME: DEBRA D. SMITH

BORN: FORT WAYNE, IN

COSTUME: CHRISTMAS HAROLDERS
(GREEN) 1994
GREGG BARNES

NAME: MICHELLE GAUDETTE

BORN: NASHUA, NH

COSTUME: RED, WHITE, & BLUE POOF 1981
FRANK SPENCER

NAME: SAE LA CHIN

BORN: SEOUL, SOUTH KOREA

COSTUME: GOLD & RHINESTONES 1977
FRANK SPENCER

NAME: LISA-MARIE LEWIS

BORN: VANCOUVER, BRITISH COLUMBIA

COSTUME: SILVER FEATHER FINALE 1990
ERTÉ

NAME: ANNA RICHARDSON

BORN: COLUMBUS, OH

COSTUME: GOLD TUXEDO 1982
MICHAEL CASEY

NAME: SHERI FALCONER

BORN: ORANGE COUNTY, CA

COSTUME: RED FIREWORKS 1981
FRANK SPENCER

NAME: DANIELLE JOLIE DALE

BORN: CHICAGO, IL

COSTUME: WHITE TAILS 1979
PETE MENEFEE

NAME: Melissa Rouse-Stuart

BORN: Pittsburgh, PA

COSTUME: Gershwin Boa 1990
Erté

NAME: Jaime Fisher

BORN: Columbus, NE

COSTUME: Flame 1984
Frank Spencer

NAME: Jessica Perrizo

BORN: Fargo, ND

COSTUME: Sailor 1984
Michael Casey

THE 1940s

After the attack on Pearl Harbor, the United States entered World War II. The Rockettes joined the USO and traveled abroad to entertain the troops. They supported the wartime effort by traveling across the United States as well. They were involved in wartime shows at the Copacabana, the Army Air Corps base in Pawling, New York, and at the Stage Door Canteen.

The Rockettes and Eleanor Roosevelt even hosted a War Bond Rally at Madison Square Garden.

The Rockettes perform for the U. S. troops.

The Rockettes continued to do regular shows at the
Music Hall, but a troupe of eight dancers ventured out
to perform for Army Air Corps, and made other special
appearances in New York.

COSTUME DESIGN

The Rockettes' costumes have dazzled audiences through the years. Some of the greatest designers of the day have created costumes for the legendary dance troupe, including Bob Mackie, Erté, and Vincente Minnelli.

Vincente Minnelli was one of the first costume and set designers. He became one of Hollywood's finest directors, husband of Judy Garland and father of Liza Minnelli.

The Father of the Art Deco style, Erté, designed elaborate costumes for the Rockettes that seem to be an extension of the Music Hall itself.

Bob Mackie, "the sultan of sequins and rajah of rhinestones," not only designs clothes for Barbie and Cher, but also costumes for the Rockettes.

Famed Broadway designers James Morcom, John William Keck, Marco Montedoro, and Frank Spencer were at one time designers for the dance troupe.

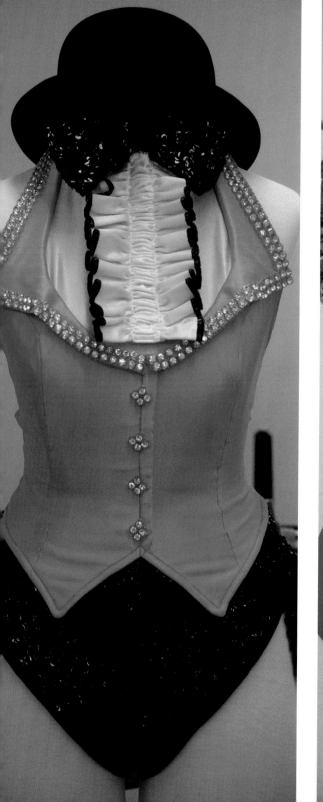

black cague

gold cloth

gold gauze

velvet

4 Rockettes

Original sketches of The Rockettes' early costumes are still used today for design inspiration and ideas.

In the early days, designers created hand-painted costume cards that seamstresses used to make the costumes.

cellophane

gabardine

Vibrant colors are a staple in creating costumes for the Rockettes

In general, costumes are fitted for each Rockette three different times, and continual alterations are required.

THE 1950s

Television replaced radio as the dominant form of mass media in the 1950s, and in 1956, the Rockettes made their television debut on *Wide Wide World*, a program that was broadcast every Sunday afternoon.

The troupe performed in the Macy's Thanksgiving Day Parade in 1957. This event is still viewed by millions of Americans each year.

With a completely new show produced every week, the Rockettes practically lived at Radio City Music Hall. There were often three shows to learn: the current performance, and rehearsals for the next two shows as well as costume fittings. The women were required to stay after the late movie to practice the next show on the Great Stage. The schedule didn't leave much time to return home to sleep or eat.

"When the Music Hall was built, Roxy insisted it should be a livable city unto itself. Incorporated into the backstage area was a twenty-six bed dormitory, a hospital staffed by a trained nurse, a cafeteria, a tailor shop, and numerous other amenities."[4]

NAME: Alicia Luciano

BORN: Byram, NJ

COSTUME: Dancing in Diamonds 1982
Bob Mackie

NAME: Ann Christen Cooley-Presley

BORN: Mackinaw City, MI

COSTUME: Christmas Harolders (Green) 1994
Gregg Barnes

NAME: Jill Wolins

BORN: Buffalo, NY

COSTUME: City Rhythm 1999
Deborah Newhall

NAME: Brittany Marcin

BORN: St. Augustine, FL

COSTUME NAME: Christmas Carousel 1989
Leeanne Mitchell

NAME: Jenelle Engleson

BORN: Fairfax, VA

COSTUME NAME: Silver Feather Finale 1990
Erté

NAME: Corinne Tighe

BORN: Plainfield, NJ

COSTUME NAME: Reindeer 1999
Gregg Barnes

NAME: ERIN BOYD-JELLISON

BORN: NEW BREMAN, OH

COSTUME: SILVER FEATHER FINALE 1990
ERTÉ

NAME: ALISON PATERSON

BORN: AUSTIN, TX

COSTUME: ORANGE MIRROR 1977
FRANK SPENCER

NAME: MEG HUGGINS

BORN: TRENTON, NJ

COSTUME: DANCING IN DIAMONDS 1982
BOB MACKIE

NAME: STEPHANIE LANG

BORN: NEW YORK, NY

COSTUME: FLAME 1984
FRANK SPENCER

NAME: MICHELLE COMBS

BORN: SEVERN, MD

COSTUME NAME: SEQUINS AND FUR (RED) 1987
PETE MENEFEE

NAME: GELSEY WEISS

BORN: AUSTIN, TX

COSTUME NAME: CHRISTMAS CAROUSEL 1989
LEEANNE MITCHELL

THE 1960s

The 1960s were a time of social change and political activism. The Rockettes' costumes have stayed true to their traditional style, but were not immune to fashion and change. In the Thirties and Forties, the dancers wore trunks that looked more like low-cut boxer shorts, but after the bikini craze entered the fashion world in the 1960s, the Rockettes raised their kicks and hemlines with increased sex appeal.

In 1961, Eastman Kodak created a color photomural featuring the Rockettes. It was the largest mural of its kind ever made, and was hung in New York City's Grand Central Terminal.

America entered the space race by the 1960s, and the Rockettes appeared on stage as astronauts.

When President Kennedy was assassinated in November of 1964, Radio City closed for a day to show respect for the fallen leader.

NAME: Amy Burnette

BORN: Great Falls, MT

COSTUME: Mirror 2003
Gregg Barnes

NAME: Megan Schenck

BORN: Versailles, KY

COSTUME: Rockette Red Santa 1982
Pete Menefee

NAME: Laura McKenzie

BORN: Kalamazoo, MI

COSTUME: White tails 1979
Frank Spencer

NAME: DONNA KAPRAL WADEWITZ

BORN: DENVILLE, NJ

COSTUME: GOLD SWIRL 2001
GREGG BARNES

NAME: JACEY LAMBROS

BORN: ONEONTA, NY

COSTUME: HAPPY FEET 1990
EDUARDO SICANGO

NAME: NIKKI WILLIAMS

BORN: ROCKLIN, CA

COSTUME: DANCING IN DIAMONDS 1982
BOB MACKIE

NAME: Carrie Janell

BORN: San Antonio, TX

COSTUME: Reindeer 1999
Gregg Barnes

NAME: Kelly Arne

BORN: New Berlin, WI

COSTUME: Gold swirl 2001
Pete Menefee

NAME: Amanda Kloots

BORN: Canton, OH

COSTUME: Bells 1987
Pete Menefee

CHRISTMAS SPECTACULAR

Every year, more than a million visitors make the Radio City Christmas Spectacular part of their holiday festivities. The eight-week show has been a sellout success since its debut. The original 1933 production was a holiday gift to the movie- going audiences. The show's legendary "Parade of the Wooden Soldiers" and the "Living Nativity" scenes were developed and choreographed by Rockettes' founder Russell Markert.

The iconic toy-soldier costumes of the Christmas Spectacular are the authentic 1933 Vincente Minnelli design, that he modeled after a porcelain doll; the outfits have remained unchanged since their debut. The costumes are specially crafted and sized for the individual Rockettes, and each takes about twelve hours to make. Although these costumes are breathtaking to behold, their intricate construction doesn't allow the dancers much freedom of movement. The hats are nearly three feet tall, the pants are stiffly starched, and the red jackets button narrow and high.

In the Living Nativity, the Rockettes abandon their eye-high kicks to present a stately living tableau of the birth of Christ.

The current ninety-minute format was launched in 1979.

Since 1994, the Christmas Spectacular has gone on the road. Now, it plays to enthusiastic audiences across the country.

The Rockettes perform the "Parade of the Wooden Soldiers" as stiffly as if they are each made of wood.

The show-stopping finale is the domino fall. A cannon blast starts the fall, and the entire line of Rockettes cascades backwards.

POWELL AND MARKET

AQUATIC PARK MARITIME MUSEUM

HYDE AND BEACH

26

SAN FRANCISCO WELCOMES THE ROCKETTES

1970s — TODAY

Radio City management began closing the theatre for weeks at a stretch, leaving the once busy Rockettes with time on their hands. The troupe petitioned for the right to take the show on the road when the Music Hall was dark. In 1977, the Rockettes appeared at Harrahs in Lake Tahoe, Nevada. Their precision dancing took the west coast by storm as they went on to play to sold-out crowds in Las Vegas.

In 1978, Radio City Music Hall was slated to close due to financial problems. The Rockettes lead the crusade to save the theatre. In 1979, the Music Hall was designated a New York City Landmark, saving it from the wrecking ball (it was designated a National Historic Landmark in 1987). The movie-and-stage-show format remained a Radio City signature until 1979, when the mass showcasing of new films called for a different focus.

The 1980s introduced the Aerobics exercise craze within America. For years, The Rockettes have shown that dancing is the way to stay fit.

In 1982, the Rockettes appeared in the movie *Annie,* playing their Depression-era sisters.

This same year, Leggs stockings used the world-famous Rockettes' legs in their hosiery commericials.

The world of sports hasn't been immune to the lure of the Rockettes' precision. In 1988, the Rockettes starred in the Super Bowl Halftime Show in San Diego, a spectacle seen by almost one billion people around the world.

2000 was a year of celebrations. Radio City Music Hall marked the seventy-fifth anniversary of the Rockettes, with more than 10,000 women having shared in the legacy by performing as a Radio City Rockette. The Rockettes also helped the New York Yankees celebrate their World Series victory.

In 2001, the Rockettes were invited to perform at President Bush's presidential inauguration in Washington, D.C., where they danced their way down the steps of the Lincoln Memorial.

In 2005, the Rockettes performed at their second presidential inauguration.

The Rockettes style is often imitated, but never equaled. The impact they have had on American culture can be measured in any small town with a dance team that attempts those famous eye-high kicks at a Friday night football halftime show. As long as there are audiences that appreciate the precision-style dance, and talented women willing to hone their dance skills, there will be a place for the Rockettes. Ladies and gentleman, the world-famous Radio City Rockettes…dancing into the future.

JAMES PORTO is an artist of immeasurable talent; his unique vision and immense technical skills have placed him in the vanguard of contemporary photography. He received a Bachelor of Science in Professional Photography degree from Rochester Institute of Technology in 1982, moved to New York City, and began working as a photo assistant. He opened his own photography studio in New York City in 1985. His specialty was producing multiple image special-effect photographs for advertising and editorial clients using elaborate darkroom and in-camera techniques before pioneering digital imaging technologies. He received a grant from New York Fellowship for the Arts to create a series of cubist images and has since exhibited his work in New York City, nationally and internationally. More recently, he participated in a group show of photography at the Rock and Roll Hall of Fame and Museum in Cleveland. He is currently represented by the Christopher Henry Gallery in New York City.

PHOTO CREDITS

p. 7 image by James Porto, pp. 8–9 George Kalinsky for Madison Square Garden, pp. 10–29 images by James Porto, p. 30 image from MSG Entertainment, pp. 32–33 image from MSG Entertainment, pp. 34–37 images by James Porto, p. 38 images from MSG Entertainment, pp. 40–41 images from MSG Entertainment, pp. 42–47 images by James Porto, p. 48 ©New York Times Pictures, p. 49 image from MSG Entertainment, pp. 50–51 images from MSG Entertainment, pp. 52–55 images by James Porto, p. 56 image from MSG Entertainment, p. 58 Jimmy Sileo, ©MSG Entertainment, p. 59 images from MSG Entertainment, p. 60 images by James Porto, pp. 62–63 images by James Porto, pp. 64–68 images from MSG Entertainment, p. 70 top left, Cosmo-Sileo, ©MSG Entertainment, top right, bottom right and left, from MSG Entertainment, p. 71 by Cosmo-Sileo, ©MSG Entertainment, pp. 72–75 images by James Porto, pp. 78–82 images by James Porto, pp. 84–87 images by James Porto, p. 88 by Cosmo-Sileo, ©MSG Entertainment, pp. 90 top, by Rob Brown, ©MSG Entertainment, bottom, by George Kalinsky for Madison Square Garden, p. 91–92 by George Kalinsky for Madison Square Garden, p. 93 top, by George Kalinsky for Madison Square Garden, bottom, by Dave Alloca, pp. 94–95 images by James Porto

ACKNOWLEDGEMENT

p. 76 The world-famous Radio City Rockettes as featured on the giant Eastman Kodak Colorama display in Grand Central Terminal, New York City.

ENDNOTES

[1] Charles Francisco, *The Radio City Music Hall An Affectionate History of the World's Greatest Theater* (New York: E. P. Dutton, 1979), 49

[2] Charles Francisco, *The Radio City Music Hall An Affectionate History of the World's Greatest Theater* (New York: E. P. Dutton, 1979), VII

[3] Charles Francisco, *The Radio City Music Hall An Affectionate History of the World's Greatest Theater* (New York: E. P. Dutton, 1979), 17

[4] Charles Francisco, *The Radio City Music Hall An Affectionate History of the World's Greatest Theater* (New York: E. P. Dutton, 1979), 69